# Figure 1

poems by

Beth McDermott

# Figure 1

Published by Pine Row Press
Ft. Mitchell, KY  41011

ISBN: 978-1-7363394-3-5

March 2022

First Edition

10  9  8  7  6  5  4  3  2  1

Cover art credit:
Angelika Piwowarczyk

Publisher's website at pinerow.com

Author's website at bethmcdermott.com

# CONTENTS

## I.

## II.

III.

# Figure 1

*You will forgive me, Sir,*
*But often on this cottage do I muse*
*As on a picture, till my wiser mind*
*Sinks, yielding to the foolishness of grief.*

–William Wordsworth, "The Ruined Cottage"

I.

# Matryoshka

This doll, painted
　　　　to resemble a peasant woman,
　　　　　　has blue eyes,

rouged cheeks, and is
　　　　wearing trumpet bell-shaped
　　　　　　poppies instead

of clothing. I read about
　　　　the morphology of the red
　　　　　　poppy, a process so

abrupt that a calyx seems *to lose*
　　　　*its identity at once,* as it has
　　　　　　here, in the outer-

most doll: only the leaves can be
　　　　called the *calyx.* But we can
　　　　　　go back: the buds

of its breasts are not so easily
　　　　lost. Designed to nest,
　　　　　　the matryoshka doll

splits, top from bottom, to reveal another
　　　　figure from the same
　　　　　　stripped block of balsa.

The eye color goes—the lower
　　　　lashes disperse like shavings.
　　　　　　Poppies fold into

themselves—how small
     can they get? The inner-
          most doll is like the calyx:

not the green leafy top,
     but the whole straw-
          berry.

## Look Away

What if I don't
open the issue? The cover

is like a portrait painting
challenging us to judge

her value. Marriable
or not marriable—

ignore that she's waiting
for a donor's

everything:
skin, muscle, jaws,

teeth, cartilage, soft palate,
blood vessels, nerves,

brows, dimple, and
cheek mole. Simply

see a static, decorative
possession that faces

the hospital window
veiled with sheers. That holds

a bouquet of roses tied
with ribbon and wears

a blush lace bell sleeve
draping her wrist.

# Like the Biologists,

I thought
the ghost orchid's labellum

split into lateral
tendrils so the giant

sphinx moth would land
between them, its twelve-

inch tongue designed to suck
from a twelve-inch

tube. But stalking the magic
of long, open legs

with help from light
and camera traps revealed

encounters I didn't know
existed. I can watch

the fig, streaked, pawpaw
or giant sphinx hover, probe,

and pollinate the ghost.

## *Figure 34*

*after Alexander Gardner*

How limited
the plate is

once the image
has been fixed.

Why is each face
hidden in the next

body's armpit
as if there's no

difference
among them?

I imagine this man
closest to

the plate edge
had the foresight

to know he'd
form a less-than

sign—
unbuttoned

britches

a tuft of pubic

hair exposed
to the lens

like a train
in a tunnel.

# Metamorphosis

She was taught to put her brother's
oxygen mask on first, so instead

of practicing Saturday yoga,
she picks him up from

the group home, bathes him, shaves
him, cuts his hair, drags him

to the lab to detect his future
and watches the phlebotomist

almost mess up. They enjoy
ice cream if he cooperates

with her caretaking, which looks
like a caterpillar digesting itself.

## *Port de bras*, or Carriage of the Arms

The arm should not move
from the elbow or the wrist.

I watch the girl make these
points disappear, as if she

has no bones but scapulae:
a monarch's forewings, wet

and crinkled. She follows
her cupped palm while her

teacher's voice repeats like
an instar: *there is a string in-*

*side of you, uncoiling like*
*a proboscis.* In the viewing

room, dimly lit so that I can
see through the half-silvered

surface, I'm still envious.

# Judgment

*Then spake the woman whose the living child was
unto the king, for her bowels yearned upon her son,
and she said, O my lord, give her the living child,
and in no wise slay it. But the other said, Let it be
neither mine nor thine, but divide it.*

—1 Kings 3:26

In Stomer's version
of the judgment

of Solomon
the true

mother looks
stripped

of her in-
fant who's

dangling by his
ankle in the guard's

hand detached
from her

exposed
breast

but don't under-
estimate the other

mother she
held on-

to her dead
son until his

blanket was a
hammock clouding

an untended
garden

## Apiosporina Morbosa

The black knot
in the chokecherry tree

started as a swelling
beneath petiole,

undetectable
when tiers

of flowers clustered
like grapes. If only

she'd had faith
that mold spores would

populate,
or questioned

the face value
of beauty—

because when the seasons
changed and leaves

buckled under
rain, the gall

was obvious: against
sky something cast

iron; against *stark—*
*silhouette*

and *disease.*

# Cedar Road

Does it matter what you carve
        from the fields? Take the road
I travel most, but circa 1873.
        Two brothers, compilers
of the atlas map, drew Cedar
        Road as if from a
daguerreotype: a horse and carriage
        passes by the residence
of the first county supervisor,
        Van Duser. The brothers
captured his bustling yard,
        barn, and kitchen garden,
pin oak towering over his pine
        grove shielding
all he loved from the other side
        of the shut front gate.

Excavators dig
        an expressway through
the corn. Midday, sunny: The dust
        is steady; the pin oak
can do nothing. Last night,
        when the moonlight
through my window backlit one
        handprint, I pressed
the glass, thinking my palm
        was a match.

## On Likeness

The features most likely
            to be recognized

by those who know me—
            hair color, eye

color, identifying scar
            between my brows—

are open
            to interpretation

if I'm found
            by excavators

in the future.
            My remains unearthed

would be conclusive proof
            that I existed,

just as Jane did
            before she starved

to death—
            twenty years younger

than I am. But digital
            bone models are

insufficient

without the artist

giving her lids without
              lashes, tooth-

pick pupils,
          nude lips.

# Give and Take

I'd describe myself as a white sea
  without a coastline; without a cliff-
side to interrupt me, I am water
  breeding water: I have no
southernmost point. But at the Cliffs
  of Moher, the crests and
troughs of each wave are chisel and
  hammer above the frothy
outline of an obelisk that's
  always being forged. Think
of the Atlantic constantly eroding
  rock shale and sandstone—
while the puffin lays its one egg
  in the same burrow as last year
and sea pinks domesticate the salt.

# Dust Pneumonia

To make the small repeated
motion of uprooting

grasses easier, one nester
mortgages the tractor

and one-way plow,
yielding bushels

of grain he can't
stop producing despite

incurable
silicosis—

*you are loaded with dirt*
the doctor explains,

prescribing
somewhere else.

## Rain Follows the Plow

Faye's father
built an orchard and

underground lake
from a small mountain

of grain. She filled their new
house with piano music.

Who cares what came
before: the hiss of a flat

iron his wife pressed
against Faye's

walls when centipede
legs scratched

the outdated newsprint.

## Cyclamen persicum

From *kýklos*—cycle. Known
for blooming when others go
dormant. Last November,
I took home a hardy one
from my local greenhouse. Then
it was in full bloom: stalks
high in the plant's dense
crown, its petals flexed
instead of splayed. Later,
a gradual nod once the stems
ripened like veins flushed
with oxygenated blood.

But this winter,
a poor showing; I think
I keep the house
too warm. A lone flower spurts
against my window: flash of
magenta. Outside,
the grass is just straw.
Swallows, settled on electric wire,
touch that and nothing else.

## The Cutting

To harness it
by distilling

its veins—
Sarah said, *You grow*

*lavender*
*to cut it.* We use

*you* to talk about
people in

general, including
the speaker and

hearer. Like
*you're making a*

*mistake*; or, *why else*
*would you grow it?*

Round-
backed bees

had opened each
minute lilac-

colored flower,
laid grains in

drawers. *You could*

*be making*

*potpourri*, Sarah
told me—

against
leaving it alone.

## Bird for Bird

But the bird hides
itself. If only I could study

the jay acting like the killdeer, who offers itself

instead of its shallow nest:
*watch me drag my fake broken*

*wing.* I'd be surprised
that watching it come undone

is distracting enough
(look how the killdeer's copper

rump is uncovered by coverts)
to believe that ivory-black

splattered eggs are stones.

# Disappearing Act

*after Vermeer's*
Officer and Laughing Girl

Because the real subject of the painting
is light, the shred of his profile

foils her face, too engaged in what he's
saying about light not being a metaphor

for time. What if she asked *where is the
density located* but couldn't respond

upper-left-shoulder into palm. Who can see
without zooming in that the real quality

of her hands is not the light falling there
but the palms daubed with it as if

reciprocity is not a thing.
The same gold cascades down

her sleeves. Are there trees outside?
You can't work around him.

II.

## After "Letters from the Dust Bowl"

*Who*
*shall say*

*if perseverance*
*is inertia*

is a question I've
asked out of fear.

Then waited for some
one to skim this

other-
wise clean water.

## Arm (Self Portrait), 1976

There are no straight lines in
Mapplethorpe's arm—

just hillocks and dry
lakes, his fingers cascading

eighth notes on a staff
opposite under-

arm hair. He is pinned
by the lens, redeeming

as the Barbados
threadsnake that sits

on a quarter. It evolved
to fill the centipede's

shoes without
proof of the species'

ecological import.

# The Partitioned Task

The first worker harvests
the seed, then hauls

her load along the trail
until she meets an

unladen ant. I learn
that this is optimal,

like a bucket brigade
transporting water versus

straining yourself.
As *Figure 1* shows,

she gives her seed without
hesitation to the next

available ant, who becomes
informed and doesn't steal it.

# Portrait of an Artist (Pool with Two Figures)

> *[The pool paintings] were about the surface of the
> water, the very thin film, the shimmering
> two-dimensionality.*
> —David Hockney

As the artist's former lover watches
     the swimmer with an intensity only
rivaled by chromium oxide,
     the toe of his loafer inches
toward the pool's edge, bowed
     head sloping like the mountains
that fade to lavender smoke-filled
     sand. Where the patio might have
extended, banana leaves issue
     a threat: sword tips backed by
mountain peaks, two redwood dagger trees—
     even the onlooker's sun-
kissed coiffure shields the swimmer's
     horizontal body from becoming
a loner ousted from the scenery.

## *Lophelia pertusa*

A wall of coral has
nothing to do

with rigs and wrecks,
or the war tanker

torpedoed by a U-
boat while delivering

90,000 pounds of
fuel oil. But the biologist

explains any hard
substrate provides

a firm base when
oases are rare. Imagine

a cauliflower
floret untouched

by trawlers
blooming white on

white, uncut.

# Mutation

After the skin cancer
was removed, I became a

pink waxy lump
cut into sections, coded

with dyes and frozen
like a layer cake.

I controlled how I
saw myself stand out:

on the sand, watching
boogie boarders

glisten with salt, different
as the spotted seatrout

that disintegrated
in the beach parking lot.

## What He Saw

When Demuth
led the poet

to his abstract portrait,
was Williams tired

of being associated
with the images

in his poems?
I imagine him

homing in on a pin-
hole, profile

reflected in
bone char and

vegetable oil.
He nodded:

the effect was
cinematic—

smoke swirled
like undiffused

light wafting
into a stagnant

room where

boys made

cigars for
men in black tie.

## The Boulder Problem Speaks to the Free-Soloist

I'm the pea-sized nub you have to
cling to while performing a split

to reach a toehold. I'm the alternative
to scaling glass-slick faces.

Remember that you twice rehearsed
the vertical slab called *Freeblast*,

and your intuition hasn't become
lunacy. You still believe in

climbing El Capitan alone,
without a rope, palming

the wall until your eyes drain
of warmth. You're prepared

for the bees, frogs, and birds
that burst from crevices

as you pop your foot to complete
your practiced choreography.

## On Containment

*A year after teams of rescuers pulled him out
of the collapsed mountain, Vega put on a
mining helmet again.*
      —Héctor Tobar, "Sixty-Nine Days"

Is he triggered
by distant rumblings,

or the moth-like
triangular shards

somehow
detached from

the swarm? Picture him,
slanted in the truck bed,

illuminated
by the other men's

lamps: no landscape reflects
the shadows of his

arms and legs so sharply as
rock corporations

are paying him to
drill. After rebuilding

his chest, so his clavicle
relaxed somewhat into

45

flesh, Vega opted
to go back—no cure

but work.

## Raised Bed

Having witnessed
the mass-planting

of *Rudbeckia hirta*
enflame and extinguish,

I think of the species
of mole with unformed

eyes that keeps a
larder of paralyzed

earthworms for sapped
days: instead of

digging, the *Talpa
occidentalis* pulls one

between its paws
for cleaning, squeezes

the pipeline empty.

# Reflection

I wanted to name your doppelganger

during our post-bath nightly ritual:

polar fleece sleeper seated on the Formica counter

whose wet straw hair I arced

back before it parted and fell, curtaining your eyes.

You'd press the panoramic

bathroom mirror as if you were the driver

taking corn ears to a feeder

house, the crushed stalks twisting into

disappearance, the ears swept by curved blades

to a spinning cage raining grain.

## *Popillia japonica*

A mere month they lived above soil
as the social versions of their former

selves: compact houses composed
of green television screens and

wood laminate floors. Imagine after
pupating, a thoughtless orgy leaving

only a lace-like skeleton of veins.
Pregnant, I woke each morning

determined to face the inevitable
clusters of slow, gluttonous

beetles eating, mating, and laying
eggs like they never lived entirely

separate from one another or
burrowed deeper for warmth.

## Equinox

He pierces the air like a dorsal
fin. He collapses on the lawn,

rolls over, towels dew, gauges
the clouds above him, sky-

writes his invisible name.
*Bring me the trowel*, I hear

myself say. Instead, his hands
cup the yellow confetti that fell

with the first hard rain. Poise and
counterpoise: the forsythia is

green. The lowest hanging branch
takes root, second windpipe, ripe

for a cutting sown elsewhere.

## Degas's *The Dance Class*, 1874

It's the ballet master's elbow we see
    mirrored in the foremost dancer's
casual second position, in the bleachers
    where the waiting girls are as
sharp-edged as the mirror-frame, poster
    frame, doorframe, or crook
of two walls' shell-colored crown molding.
    Unwittingly, these sisters
share their evergreen tree shape with
    the cityscape. But the student
who executes an arabesque or attitude
    (her leg is hidden under tulle)
knows the suggestion of *epaulement*
    is like an antique find or
swath of gild: take, she says, your cue
    from these walls brushed
a bluish eau-de-nil. This is how to
    soften the bones of the thumb,
or the whole hand—inclined to curl
    like the rose's whorl, the one
near the base of the music-score stand.

## Most People Are Familiar with Robins

First you preen as if combing smoke
from a cloud's edge—that kind of

godliness is in you, even as a *familiar
gray bird*. Then remember nothing

of this work: your wings rise and
hover, opening to a span that

a coryphée mimics when she pushes
rising water away with soft

fingertips. But then you run-and-
stop the course of my lawn, hunting

the thread that unravels us—
waiting for assistance from the wind.

## At the Historical Society Spaghetti Dinner,

I meet Lucy, who
elects to document

barns approved
for demolition: photo-

graphs that are keep-
sakes—that's all.

She doesn't enter
a barn to sample

wood cores with fifty
to one hundred

rings, simply waits
for the lit match: *click*:

then tags her photos
with neon post-

its. Her *Gone* is not
a subtle reminder;

the image raises
itself like a rotting

stump covered with
a plastic tarp.

# The Lesson

*How do we actually*
*know*, the plant clinic

director asks,
holding a symptomatic

branch she peels and knicks
for culture. The answer

radiates rust rings
that fade beneath

slush on the agar plate.
But only the microscope

confirms the requisite
whorls: *verticillate*

recalls the beauty
of liquid globules

clinging to a fishing line,
or the floating pearls

of an illusion necklace
with dead tissue for a neck.

## How to Leave a Farmhouse

Beyond the mossy stoop, flanked
by pines like stalwart weeds,

the farmland is newly hemmed
by the interstate. On it you

ascend like teeth when a mouth
opens to sing. The wind-in-your-

hair feeling is like forgetting
yourself run ragged: a kerchief

only flaps that side of the wind-
break: massive bur, understory

trees; triplets of ironwood cut out
for leverage. You'd worked in

private. Now they're everyone's
blue printed curtains, chard plantlets.

III.

## The Mushroom Farmer

She is digging her heels in
soil balled up

on the plow. The feature
story is her chance

to self-promote,
even though nothing

will save her
from eminent

domain, including
her revulsion

for starter spawn.
Yet her perspective is so

specialized—
the public can't

translate it.
Who cares

that she uses
manure, which stems

from *maneuver?*
Here she is

among the fruiting

bodies, shining

her lamp over racks
of shitake.

Their spores require
such sterility—

a room like a cave
with the ground

swept clean.

## Ride

Is it stupid to declare I'm hopelessly devoted
when my beliefs always come full

circle? One minute I defend you, the next
I'm riding in a Ferris Wheel gondola, correlating

my shifting perspective with the shift
in my apparent weight. When I feel buoyant,

you're a chit, tile, chip, token, peg, meeple or
marker—a game piece I can push

around the board. I'm the centripetal force
that constrains you to the path of least

resistance, until I slow like the first
wheel dynamited into scrap.

## How to splice modern day with an extinct species like the passenger pigeon?

No footage exists
    of the 850

square miles of nesting
    sites becoming

a weather system
    at the mercy of

rakes and pitchforks.
    All I know is that

wild pigeons
    plundered grain,

then succumbed
    to the telegraph

and railroad. So, I study
    swarm behavior:

how they came in
    off the water

following three
    basic rules

for how to be
    unoriginal:

*stay close,*
　　*synchronize*

*your movements, avoid*
　　*collision.*

## Constructing Audubon's *The Birds of America*

The first time he stooped
       to observe a specimen of

*American robin* or *migratory*
       *thrush* in the lower half

of a *Prunus caroliniana*, Audubon
       had left his rifle at home.

He took notes: the female was gray-
       headed and occupied

with breakfast; her breast was a
       duller orange than the dark-

headed male's, and their un-
       fledged young were white-

throated. But instead of describing
       how the male's tail fanned

when he dropped down to feed
       chicks meant to be kept hidden,

Audubon wrote *star top, column.*
       He marked an x on his map,

left for his gun, and went back.

## Strip-Mall Bakery

Is it sufficient
to grieve for an image—

not the thing
itself? We're all standing on

black and white checkered
vinyl, over land altered by

glaciers. *In the first
stages, so-called break*

*rollers crack the kernel
open.* The children smudge

a case of assorted
donuts. I spent my

childhood looking at braided
spikelets in rapid

succession. A field of corn
was impenetrable—

left my own body.

## Portend, Not Pretend

Toss yarrow
stalks, dole

out my lots.
Find a rabbit's

shoulder blades
to watch.

Heed earth-
quakes and

lighting, know
what the dead

know: the true
number of

moons, their
rivers,

our crows.

# Pentimenti

Except for the faint outline
of a second ear,

Caravaggio reworked
nothing about

*The Taking of Christ*,
using pure lead

white so you're caught
beneath the soldier's

gilded leather glove, reflected
in the highly polished

metal opposite
the flames made

by a billowing
cloak. How would you feel

subjected to such
scrutiny, illuminated

by the chiaroscuro
of multiple furrowed

objects? Forget Judas
gripping your shoulder

like a worried brother.

# Emergency Action Plan

A pair of mallards settle into the approach channel
like a family taking a flume ride at Logger's Run.

I'm standing between water intake and outlet
structures,
parallel with a reservoir I envision flooding

*potential inundation zone based on PIN
Number as of March 1985.* I cross the half-solid,

half-dotted artery labeled *Embankment
and Spillway* before the sinuous segment

runs like a fissure through a blood-filled
breach. What hasn't seeped through the concrete

joints swills in my memory. But on the map
legend, the deeper blue floodplain denotes

a decreased flood risk the closer water gets
to my kitchen window, where I observe

the ducks' different behaviors depending on
rainfall: today, they're luge sledding, but

yesterday I saw them wrestle breast to breast.

## Pull the Wool Away

Why did I drive here
except for a purely

visual experience
that can't hold

sun low and yellow
as a yolk

whisked over
ruminant cattle

excreting methane
I breathe in

and expel
thinking

*What's the farmer*
*feeling*

as he frees
his goat from

the woven wire

# Can You Be Present

*after* U-060 *by Jerry Takigawa*

Imagine using this photograph
to wax ethereal. Cutting it
with your eye is like paring
an apple, eating the endocarp
and spitting out seeds.

Can you be fully present
while you interpret that
the artist who scattered bundles
of pine needles didn't wrap
each fascicle like the filmy
waist of a chiffon skirt.

Can you accept how fire
starters, mulch makers, nest
builders and composters
unraveled crepe yarn to build
an arch—that, when lifted,
the speckled eggs would
float against the silk.

# Crisis

*This, too,* my mother says, *shall pass.* Meaning
not what was averted but what will be short-
lived. *This:* a cornucopia of dust and pill-
boxes—still-life on the nightstand she
swipes off. Replaces it with tinkling ice,
straw like concertina wire. Something there is
that does love a wall, patiently waiting to hear
what ails. So, when she finds the loophole,
she'll be there, my mother says, *lock-stock-
and-barrel. I'll be there with corkscrew
and hammer.* She's practiced the art of closing
remarks, leavens her bread so my joints
dovetail. In the embankment, she shovels snow.

## The Ongoing Moment

*Never before had he encountered women such as
these. Stroop ran forward, declaring, 'Indeed, these
are the true partisans!'*
—Dan Porat, The Boy: A Holocaust Story

Beyond the frame lines,
      the remnant refusing voluntary
resettlement is aflame in pockets
      of resistance—pistol-wielding females

      with grenades in
their underpants are ripe for
      photographing, except
their weapons aren't here. Only pearls strung

around one woman's neck,
      her godet skirt and newsboy cap
conflict a viewer about her
      virtue: is she victim

      or partisan? Even beyond Stroop's
report, a haunted
      man calls her *Mona Lisa*
as if her far-off look isn't practically-

minded: who is he going
      to shoot? Here, pressure bottles up,
and the patch hovering near
      the actual image

      collides like wood with her friend's

neurocranium. Zero-shaped hands blur
the frame lines, generous to include
fishtail braid and narrow boots.

## Still Life

If you ask how to photograph
flying birds, the advice is
to pan at the same speed
as they're flying.
So that must mean
that stationary things
deserve our lock and stare.
But what happens when you're
the one moving as if stop-
and-go down a city street,
and you catch in your periphery
something still?

You have to twist and pan it; pan
with no zoom, pan so that the boy
I see at the corner of Harrison
is only about to cry under
the hospital sign—or could he be
simply lost? Like a coin
tossed up to decide
whose ball it is next, a flock of
blackbirds flashes silver
when it flips, end
over end. Look at his arms
as you're passing,
his arms too long
for his unfinished height.

# When I was young I, too, read *Charlotte's Web*

I think of being young whenever I hear
cilantro called *coriander*. Try it, and you

will think of Fern at the county fair. But
having grown, would she have picked

the milking stool over the Ferris wheel?
The gusset over the top-stitch, the wall over

the open air? Someday, I'll smile and say,
*When you were young we read together.*

You'll pour tea. I'll sit. Outside a finch
will prattle. Imagine us, and you will think

of water draining through a colander. If
pressed to choose, always read what I read.

## On Stieglitz's *Apples and Gable, Lake George*

At first glance, I thought

*cherries.* But that's the difference

between drupes and pomes—

not a matter of size, but of framing

their weight. Cherries cluster.

Instead, each of the four staggered

apples dangles with the force

of attraction to earth. But gravity,

for him, was easy—look how he

manipulated aperture,

collapsing the distance

between foreground and background,

apples and gable. Think of the tide

bringing in a sound wave

long after a note is struck.

### On Metaphor in the *Rural Historic Structural Survey of New Lenox Township*

Thanks to Wiss,
Janney, Elstner

and Associates,
I can spot

a spindle work porch
and jig-

saw cut trim. But PIN
08-36-200-

015 *is a structure
in crisis*; their nod

to public perception
*(while to some*

*it may appear as an
abandoned wreck)*

suggests they've
imagined

wood beneath artificial
siding

and switch
metaphors:

*sufficient historic fabric
remains.* Why try

to regain
what can't ever be

recovered?
Before the artist

arranged photo-
degraded plastic

caps in rows like
avocado rolls,

an albatross had
ingested them.

# Getting Ready

My neighbor is hanging plastic
eggs on trees with colorless

monofilament. She separates
an egg and threads both ends

of the cut line into an air hole
that prevents bursting—

knots the ends, clicks the egg
shut, and transfers the loop

from her hand to a bare branch
of her ornamental sapling as

a jeweler slips a pendant over
the velvet display bust. The egg

is suspended in air. She says
it's for the kids; and I hear *no*

*Christmas lights last year,*
*not even an inflatable Santa.*

I recall loose papers stamped
with sleet-wet boot prints,

my backseat decorated with
two dangling child's legs.

# Coeur à la Crème

I stumble upon
a stranger's blog:

this photo of the soft-
set ricotta heart

plated with tea-
spoonfuls of rasp-

berry sauce; she
holds her face

close to the plate
expecting

admirers of a quiet
sieve bruised

ruddy at the pith.

# Pink Remnant

Behind the row of swollen
Scotch pine, a farmhouse.
Blackbirds on the rooftop wait:
each is the stitch I tug

into a gaping sky. I've heard
that in winter, all it takes
is one pipe—its slow
frozen crackle. A steady

expanse at the expense
of its container: pyramidal
shape that contorts and
curtseys, or a pine that is not

harvested early. *(If you do
have a snag, never use a razor to
remove the thread.)* Christmas
tree growers lop female

flowers off to retain shape.
Before the row of swollen
Scotch pine—leader after
leader grew crooked—

this farm's toilet, cradled
in a ditch. Candy pink in the coal-
colored slush. Watch
the garbage truck not take it.

## Under Pressure

As movers load the upright piano
onto a dolly, a cloudy ring from

my teacher's ice water glass
recalls "Aragonaise," from the opera

*Le Cid.* I would have rather danced
the ballet than played it. She

would have rather performed
than taught. So, she would twist

the tip of her yellow mechanical
pencil and prescribe hours of

practice. I advanced like rotting fruit.
She wept bitterly like Chimène,

who had once tattooed *laugh and play*
onto my eight-year-old knuckles

and still allowed me to be who I was.

## Notes

"Dust Pneumonia" and "Rain Follows the Plow" are inspired by *The Worst Hard Time* by Timothy Egan.

The end of "On Metaphor in the *Rural Historic Structural Survey of New Lenox Township*" alludes to *False Food*, a series of photographs by Jerry Takigawa.

# Acknowledgements

Grateful acknowledgement is made to the editors of the following publications, in which some of these poems, at times in earlier versions, first appeared:

*Bayou:* "Equinox"

*Consilience:* "Popillia japonica"

*Harpur Palate:* "At the Historical Society Spaghetti Dinner," and "Pink Remnant"

*Jet Fuel Review:* "Crisis" and "Coeur à la Crème"

*Memorious:* "Under Pressure"

*Pine Row:* "Reflection"

*So to Speak:* "Judgment"

*Southern Humanities Review:* "Degas's *The Dance Class,* 1874"

*Storm Cellar:* "Strip-Mall Bakery"

*Terrain.org:* "Matryoshka," "Bird for Bird," and "Constructing Audubon's *The Birds of America*"

*The Hopper:* "Raised Bed"

*The Literary Bohemian:* "Give and Take"

*The National Poetry Review:* "How to Leave a
Farmhouse" and "Getting Ready"

*Thimble Literary Magazine:* "The Boulder Problem
Speaks to the Free-Soloist"

*Tupelo Quarterly:* "Dust Pneumonia," "Rain Follows
the Plow," "Disappearing Act," "After 'Letters from
the Dust Bowl,'" "On Containment," and "The
Ongoing Moment"

*Watershed Review:* "Most People Are Familiar with
Robins"

"Cedar Road," "When I was young I, too, read
*Charlotte's Web,*" and "On Stieglitz's *Apples and Gable,
Lake George*" appeared in *Off Channel,* an anthology
published by Midwest Writing Center Press.

Some of these poems previously appeared in *How to
Leave a Farmhouse,* a chapbook published by
Porkbelly Press.

Sincere gratitude to Hank Hudepohl and Pine Row
Press.

Thanks to my students and colleagues at the
University of St. Francis, the *RHINO* poetry
community, and the editorial team at *Cider Press
Review,* especially Karen Duys, Kevin Spicer, Anna
Ioanes, Virginia Bell, Naoko Fujimoto, Ralph
Hamilton, Valerie Wallace, and Caron Andregg.

Profound thanks to Virginia Konchan, Jennifer
Moore, Christina Pugh, John Sibley Williams, and
Wyn Cooper for thinking with me about the poems in
this book.

Special thanks to Hadara Bar-Nadav and Simone
Muench for their knowledge and friendship, and to
Rebecca Morgan Frank for her keen editorial insight.

Thanks to Amy Erb, Kara Nikischer, Ken and Cathy
Lomasney for their love and support.

Finally, all gratitude for Will, Liam, and Norah
McDermott.

# About the Author

Beth McDermott's poetry appears in *Pine Row, Tupelo Quarterly, Terrain.org,* and *Southern Humanities Review.* Reviews and criticism about art and ecology appear in *American Book Review, After the Art, Kenyon Review Online,* and *The Trumpeter.* She's an Assistant Professor of English at the University of St. Francis and recipient of a Distinguished Teaching Award, an Illinois Speaks Micro-Grant, and first place in the Regional Mississippi Valley Poetry Contest. She is editor-in-chief at *Cider Press Review* and lives with her family in the southwest suburbs of Chicago.

Made in the USA
Middletown, DE
11 June 2022

66859262R00050